Bad Things, Good Companies

Bad Things,
Good Companies:

A Crisis Communications Handbook

By Matthew Montague

Lulu.com

For more information,

    Matthew Montague

    95 Brown Road

    Ithaca, NY 14850

    e-mail: mattmontague@earthlink.net

Contents

What is crisis communications?

Crisis communications is the response to any unexpected public event that can adversely affect an organization's image or brand through negative media attention. In short, bad things that happen to good companies. Types of crisis include:

- Product - product recalls, regulatory crackdowns, defective products, and service interruptions.

- Organization – environmental issues, government investigation, controversial law suit, protest, strike, insider trading scandal, theft (ideas or physical assets), embezzlement, hostile takeover, death of or serious injury to top executive, criminal action by top management, natural disaster, plane crash, fire, explosion, immediate environmental hazard, related crisis (such as competitor crisis) which requires a response, false advertising accusation, celebrity spokesperson in scandal, and production sourcing internationally or at a non-union facility.

- Workforce – layoffs, work-related accidents and deaths, plant closings, accusation of discrimination based on race, sexual preference or gender, serious injury to someone within or outside of the organization, physical violence between co-workers, sexual harassment case, crime on premises, and union grievances.

The risk to the organization from these events has grown. The proliferation of news sources has created a voracious appetite for new material. The advent of the Internet and other electronic news outlets allows any situation, no matter how minor, to explode almost instantly into the local, regional, or national attention.

These two factors significantly raise the risk organizations face in their day-to-day operations, threatening to destroy in a matter of hours an image, a brand, and a reputation that took years to build.

Too often, organizations respond to these emergencies in a haphazard and irrational manner. "Circle the wagons," "deny everything," and "the press is the enemy" are innate defense mechanisms, not sane options.

However, in the adrenalin rush of cascading events, these are often easy, if incorrect, choices. The results are dismal: emotional, contradictory statements tumble out haphazardly to bewilder and embitter the press corps; leaks and rumors proliferate; the public is misled, confused, fearful, and resentful; and the corporation's value and reputation are savaged in the equity markets and in the court of public opinion.

Handled improperly, what was just a potential crisis or minor incident can become a full-blown disaster. In many cases, it is not much of an exaggeration to say that the organization itself caused most of the problem.

Bad things happen; but bad public relations doesn't have to. To counter this risk, organizations should create a plan for communications in the event of an adverse event to allow for a rapid, reasoned response.

This plan should:

- Provide overall guidelines for corporate behavior;
- Explore potential emergencies and define responses;
- Assemble a team of leaders, identify a spokesperson, and describe their roles;
- Identify necessary facilities, personnel, and equipment;
- Lay out procedures for a complete crisis response, including guidelines and checklists; and
- Provide for after-action reports, lessons learned, and plan rehearsals and revisions.

The business value of crisis communications planning

- Preserve corporate market value.

- Maintain market share.

- Preserve reputation for new customers, employees, partners, etc.

- Reduce liability (the insurance company may even pay for the service in the event of an emergency and adjust premiums if plan is in place).

This is not a plan

This handbook is <u>not</u> a crisis communications plan. The unique character of each organization makes such a generic model useless.

This guide applies industry best practices and our own experience to describe a plan, includes appendices for further definition, provides a sample plan taken from an actual corporate crisis, and is completed by a workbook public relations and corporate communications personnel can use to develop their own crisis communications plan (body sentences in italics refer to sections in the workbook).

General guidelines for crisis communications

Do the right thing.

If there is one maxim for crisis communications, and crisis response in general, it is "do the right thing." Focusing the response away from the organization and toward bringing the crisis under control, caring for those affected by the emergency, and dealing with the aftermath will leave little or no time for the attempted cover-ups and obfuscations that get organizations into trouble.

If there is one thing to remember when developing and communicating your response, it is to do the right thing – tell it all, tell it fast, and tell the truth. This altruistic approach will pay great dividends, short-term and in the long run.

There may be internal opposition to this approach. Defense mechanisms are powerful things, and the first reaction to the emergency may be a series of denials – of the extent of the emergency, of the impact on people, and of culpability.

In this litigation-crazed business environment, these may even seem to be responsible responses that safeguard the company and personal position. However, it is possible to accept responsibility without accepting liability.

Liability is not admitted when you say publicly that you are sorry someone has been injured, you are investigating the cause of that injury, and plan to do what is possible to prevent the injury in the future. The study of crisis communications repeatedly reveals that it is not the poor action that draws the fire, it is the poor reaction.

Consider two well-known cases: the Tylenol tampering and the Exxon Valdez oil spill. In the first case, Tylenol announced the emergency quickly, was concerned with and took care of the victims, and took steps to ensure that the problem would not recur. In the second, Exxon denied the extent of the disaster, blocked reporting, and fought culpability and clean-up costs, as well as new regulations on oil tanker bottoms. Which corporation did better? What was the cost of a poor response?

Over time, the long-term damage to a corporation's reputation and value will outweigh the short-term gain from a cover-up.

Finally, remember that a situation that starts out badly may turn out well. Think of the coal miners in Pennsylvania trapped in their mine a few years past. What began as a bad story, a mine collapse, transitioned to a good story, a heroic rescue.

Doing the right thing, then, is critical to protecting the integrity and reputation, not to mention the long-term value, of the company.

Overall, remember to be:

- **Honest** – "what a tangled web we weave…" Dishonesty costs credibility and shadows the truth when it is (and will be) revealed.
- **Correct** – "just the facts, ma'am…" Never say anything not known to be a fact; supposition and even honest estimates will be remembered while qualifiers will not.
- **First** – the first version of the story is the one remembered.
- **Consistent** – nothing confuses like confusion.
- **Clear** – make a plain report and don't hide behind jargon.
- **Caring** – the victims are the ones the public is concerned about, not the organization.

1. *Develop and write down a general policy for crisis communications.*

Planning

Earlier, we defined a crisis as unexpected; how do you plan for the unexpected? Three ways:

- survey your vulnerabilities and prepare responses;

- assemble a competent team to manage the crisis and define their roles; and

- identify the facilities and equipment needed for the response.

Every task done now will be one already done when time is critical, leaving more time for a reasoned, responsible response. Moreover, simply the exercise of planning and thinking through these scenarios, and assembling the team and facilities, will pay dividends despite the unpredictable nature of the actual event.

Scenarios

Every organization has their vulnerabilities. The examples listed in the front of this document provide a good, but general, list of potential problems. However, each organization's unique business, geographic position, economic impact, and products and services create a distinctive set of scenarios. Crisis planners should use the organization's safety planning, workforce, product, and organizational history, competitors' and market histories, and local history to develop their own list of probable scenarios.

1. Assemble a list of probable situations that would require a public response.

Each of these scenarios involves a different set of interested parties, or stakeholders. For instance, a financial crisis might not interest the local neighborhood while a chemical spill certainly would. A full list of possible stakeholders might include victims, employees, customers, media, government contacts, community contacts, investors and stockholders, and vendors (see appendix A for a list of suggestions).

2. For each scenario, develop contact lists that identify these stakeholders and their respective communications channels to speed response and ensure its completeness.

Take each scenario and develop it further by working through the situation's potential progress and outcomes. For instance, an accident on a manufacturing line would require assistance to the victims and their families, but also might affect safety procedures, require a government inspection, concern employees and potential employees, have implications for perceived product value, and involve repair costs.

Exploring these ramifications shows a need to communicate to the victims, interested local media, the government, employees, trade media, customers, and the financial community. During your investigation, document practices and policies already in place that reduce risk.

3. Work through each scenario and create a "package" to speed response.

Each scenario's package should include:

- A draft position and key messages;
- A draft statement (see appendix B for a sample);
- Lists of key stakeholders for the scenario and their contact information;
- Anticipated questions and answers;
- Third-party experts (and contact information); and
- A fact sheet on the operation or process involved, including schematics and photos.

Early warning signs often become apparent while organizing the response to a particular scenario. For instance, extreme cold weather may increase the likelihood of a certain type of production mishap or a certain interest rate may impact the organization's financial stability. It is prudent to note these issues and assign people to monitor to them to improve preparation and speed response.

The crisis communication team

The crisis communication team is a set of organizational leaders chosen for their expertise in a functional area and their ability to think clearly and make difficult decisions under stress. The role of each team member should be clearly defined in the crisis communications plan to avoid overlap and conflict. There should be a core team, which can then be supplemented for the particular situation.

A typical team and possible roles might include:

- CEO – team leader, convene meetings, coordinate team activities, approve release of information;
- Senior public relations manager – oversee all communications activities, and focus on external communications and especially media relations;
- Vice-presidents or members of the executive team – provide insight or expertise specific to the situation;
- Marketing director – responsible for customer communications;
- Senior manager from the affected area – provide insight specific to the cause, effects, and resolution of the situation;
- Safety and/or security officer – provide input on security issues, ongoing safety concerns, control of the scene and the facility in general;
- Human resources – handle employee communications, family notification (if necessary), and provide information about affected employees;
- The organization's legal counsel – advise on legal issues; and
- Others with important, related information, such as eyewitnesses.

4. Assemble a team of senior managers for the crisis communications team; their job is to apply the general guidelines and crisis communications plan to devise a public response to the crisis.

The crisis communications plan must have a recall roster with complete contact information for each member of this team, including work, home, cellular, and pager telephone numbers, as well as IM and e-mail addresses. Moreover, an alternative should be identified for each member of the team and their information included in the crisis communications plan.

5. Ensure that a recall roster for the crisis communications team is in the plan and up-to-date.

As the communications team devises a response, it is the responsibility of the senior public affairs manager to ensure its prompt and complete execution.

In this regard, the senior public affairs manager and his or her team should:

- Direct the work related to the release of information to the media, public, and partners;
- Produce and distribute media advisories and news releases;
- Review and approve all materials for release to media and public;
- Obtain required clearance of materials for release to media;
- Manage the response to media requests and inquiries;
- Develop and maintain media contact lists and call logs;
- Oversee media monitoring system and reports;
- Be familiar with incident and up-to-date on the situation;
- Ensure that resources are available (people, equipment, and supplies).
- Support spokespersons;
- Manage the public response via telephone, in writing, or by e-mail;
- Organize and manage, with the webmaster, the emergency response web site; and
- Oversee response to employees, investors, and other special stakeholders.

6. The public affairs staff is responsible for executing the decisions of the crisis communications team.

Spokesperson

The crisis communications team should designate an individual to represent the organization as its spokesperson, as well as a back-up spokesperson. Having a single voice for the organization increases credibility and consistency, as well as providing a representative "face" for the public. This person will make official statements and answer media questions throughout the crisis. Additional individuals, such as a financial expert, an engineer, or a leader in the community, can speak as technical experts or advisors under the auspices of the spokesperson.

The spokesperson should be:

- As senior as possible, preferably the CEO ("the buck stops there" with the public).
- Skilled in speaking with the media and staying on message in front of crowds and cameras;
- Able to speak clearly and simply, without using jargon;
- Respectful of the role of the reporter;
- Knowledgeable about the organization and the crisis at hand;
- Credible with the media and able to project confidence to the audience;
- Suitable in regard to diction, appearance and charisma;
- Sincere, straightforward and believable;
- Accessible to the media and to internal communications personnel who will facilitate media interviews; and
- Able to remain calm in stressful situations.

The senior public relations manager may substitute for the spokesperson for ordinary press briefings. However, the designated spokesperson should be at the podium when possible and for all significant announcements. Depending on the nature of the situation, other parties, such as police, fire and emergency officials, may also address the media. It is important to identify these spokespersons early in the situation to coordinate media contact.

7. Designate a spokesperson and a back-up to represent the organization throughout the situation.

Facilities

Identifying facilities and equipment required to handle a communications crisis is critical to a smooth and rapid response. It is of no use to find a room for the media, only to discover that the reporters pass the room set aside for victims and their families on the way to the coffee machine. Likewise, reporters will need telephones, fax machines, and refreshments to function during the situation; having these at hand saves time and tempers when both may be in short supply.

Crisis communications planners should designate a:

- crisis command center, set in a quiet private area, away from the rooms designated for media, familes, etc. with computers and a good, high-speed printer, multiple telephone and fax lines and equipment, and network and internet connections.

- press conference room and media center at the site but away from the center of the action, with telephone, fax, and internet connections (not via the internal network, if possible), nearby restrooms, tables and chairs, a lectern, food and coffee, and multiple electrical outlets.

- Family room for victim recovery and counselling, and for their families, set well away from the media room. If circumstances warrant, family members should be asked if they would like to have a member of the clergy present. If possible, local clergy of the same denomination should be asked to assist (create a representative contact list of local clergy).

8. Identify a command center, a press center, and a family center, as well as required equipment and resources.

Response

Declaring a crisis

A crisis can be easily identified in the case of a major accident or incident, or it can creep up, as in the case of a criminal investigation. Regardless, declaring a crisis should be the result of a careful assessment of the situation and the expected media and public interest. Identifying and declaring a crisis is the responsibility of senior management and the senior public relations manager. When a crisis is declared, the crisis communications team should be assembled immediately to:

- activate the plan;
- create a fact sheet using only the known facts of the situation – the who, why, when, where, what; and
- develop a position on the situation.

1. Activate the plan, recall and assemble the team, create a fact sheet, and develop a position on the situation.

Developing a position

In developing a position, it is difficult, but very necessary, to step outside of the organization and to view the crisis from the eye of the stakeholders. Consider which facts are most important in their eyes and what sort of expectations the public has in this situation and identify the key message of the statement. Do not speculate or release uncertain information. Use the fact sheet and a template to develop a clear, concise, and straightforward press release about the situation. Release the statement as soon as possible to the press, either live in a press conference or via fax, e-mail, or read over the telephone.

2. Use the fact sheet and the positioning to write, clear, and release a brief, factual statement about the situation.

Prepare for the media

Use this statement to communicate internally as well – to employees and to all who deal with the public such as switchboard operators, security and safety personnel. Switchboard operators should direct press calls to the command center; security and safety personnel should direct media personnel to the media center. Press escorts should be notified and sent to parking lots to meet media members.

Determine the media interest in the situation. If necessary and appropriate, schedule a press conference where the designated spokesperson will read the statement and take a number of questions. Alert the media to the time and place of the press conference.

3. Determine media interest and the appropriate responses.

The press conference

Few things create more stress for corporate executives that the press conference. This need not be so. Remember, the organization is communicating; the press is reporting what the organization communicates. Control the message and you control the coverage. Nonetheless, it is important to train corporate executives, and especially the spokesperson in media relations.

Define what kind of event you are having. News conferences are held to announce something for the first time. Press availabilities are held simply to make individuals available to answer questions or demonstrate something. Don't call unnecessary news conferences or availabilities; make sure the news is worth the media's time. Try to give the media some details of what you will be announcing before the event.

It is critical to prepare anyone speaking to the press with sample tough questions and answers and general guidelines for communicating in a crisis situation immediately before every press conference, especially as the story evolves.

Other spokespersons from official agencies may be involved, depending on the nature of the situation. Work with them to coordinate who will convey which information; they know the rules that bear on their particular area (ie. what information should be released about a defendant). It is preferable to have the organization's spokesperson begin the conference with the prepared statement, introduce others to add more information, and then finish with a short question and answer session.

Have printed materials available, including copies of the statement, a press fact sheet (not the internal version), and appropriate collateral for more information. Also include relevant schematics or descriptions of the processes involved, photographs of the equipment and location, and even a similar piece of equipment for a demonstration. Providing your visuals may keep the media from seeking out their own.

4. Use the press conference checklist (appendix X) to prepare; ensure you rehearse expected questions and answers, review guidelines, and coordinate release of information among the parties involved.

Questions to expect at the press conference include:

- What is your (spokesperson's) name and title?
- What happened?
- When did it happen?
- Where did it happen?
- What do you do there?
- Who was involved?
- Why did it happen? What was the cause?
- What are you going to do about it?
- Was anyone hurt or killed? What are their names?
- How much damage was caused?
- What effect will it have on production and employment?
- What safety measures were taken?
- Who is to blame?
- Do you accept responsibility?
- Has this ever happened before?
- What do you have to say to the victims?
- Is there danger now?
- Will there be inconvenience to the public?
- How much will it cost the organization?
- When will we find out more?

Some guidelines to remember include:

- Describe only the known facts of the situation and show concern for the public and for your employees.
- Be careful with risk comparisons -- true risk and perceived risk can be quite different. The source of the risk can be as troubling as the degree of risk. Be careful not to compare a high outrage, low hazard risk to a low outrage, high hazard risk. Bioterrorism is, for most people, is high outrage and low hazard. It can't be compared with a low outrage, high hazard risk like driving a car.

- Don't over-reassure – a high estimate of harm modified downward is much more acceptable to the public than a low estimate of harm modified upward.

- Qualify the good news – as an example, "the firefighters are still on the scene, however, their latest report is that the fire is out."

- Don't speculate – if you don't know, say so, and promise to find out.

- Be consistent – research shows that bad news doesn't cause panic; conflicting messages from authority causes panic.

- Acknowledge the danger –when people are afraid, the worst thing to do is pretend they're not. The second worst is to tell them they shouldn't be afraid.

- Give people things to do. Anxiety is reduced by action and a restored sense of control.
    - you must do X
    - you should do Y
    - you can do Z

- Don't use humor – ever.

- Rebut a rumor without really repeating it. For example, the question "word is that more than 100 have died in the factory" could be answered "we don't have casualty figures yet, but the total staff of the factory is 100, and about 50 were in the plant at the time of the accident." Limit the rebuttal to the places where the rumor exists.

- Don't volunteer information unless it is a point the company wants to make and the question hasn't been asked.

- Stay on message:
    - "What's important is to remember…"
    - "I can't answer that question, but I can tell you…"
    - Before I forget, I want to tell your viewers…"
    - "Let me put that in perspective…"

- Speak slowly and carefully. Stay in control and slow the press down; they are under pressure, but so are you. Take one question at a time, restate the question, and ask if your restatement is correct. if you are emotionally overwhelmed, angry or sad, don't be afraid to put up your hands, take a moment to collect yourself, and begin again.

- There is a limit to your role. To exceed that limit is a mistake.

Media guidelines

It is important to remember three principles when working with the media: they have a job to do; they will trust you until you lie to them and then never more; and they are interested in their story, not yours. Working within these guidelines will make your job and theirs vastly easier and the relationship between the two parties much better.

Some general guidelines to remember:

- Don't change the rules during the crisis – whether from before the situation and during the situation – unless safety considerations dictate otherwise. If media need escorts, then they always need escorts. Changes will be seen by the media as an attempt to hide things.
- If the situation is located in a very dangerous or remote location, consider pool reporting. The media on-site elect a rotating, representative team (usually a reporter, a photographer, a radio newsperson, and a television videographer and news producer) to take notes and film for the use of all. It is better to explain the situation and ask the media on-site if a pool would be acceptable.
- You cannot restrict the right of reporters to interview anyone they wish – and they will, off grounds if need be. It is better, rather, to assemble a representative group of interviewees for the media to work with on-site. This makes the reporters' jobs easier and helps to control the message.
- Treat all media equally. No leaks, no scoops, no "off the record," and no retribution.

Some guidelines for particular types of situations include:

- Do not use language that implies guilt when discussing a criminal act. For example, you can say that an employee reported sexual harassment and that we are investigating the charges.
- In case of fire or other damage to facilities, the media typically will want to know the amount of damages. Unless the insurance expert is on-site and has provided an official report, the best answer is that you cannot say at this time.

- When death or injury occurs, law enforcement officials have responsibility for notifying next-of-kin. The human resources manager should cooperate with these agencies to provide information about the individual and their next-of-kin. After it has been confirmed that next-of-kin have been notified, the organization may (but not must) release the following information: name, job title, date employed, spouse, children's names and ages, and parents. The CEO should approve release of this information.

- Photographers should be escorted immediately to the site of on-going fires so they can take pictures of the event. Law enforcement officials will cordon off the area where firefighters are working, and photographers will not be allowed inside burning buildings.

- Law enforcement officials generally will cordon off the sites of criminal investigation and not allow reporters or photographers in.

Communicating internally

Communicating to internal stakeholders is as important as communicating with the press. If your employees, vendors, investors, and customers don't feel like insiders, they are going to act like outsiders.

Use your lists of key stakeholders to identify those affected by the crisis and your public statements to develop messages for each audience. Consider how the organization's web site and intranet site might be used to deliver and maintain the currency of this information (see appendix X for more information on Internet crisis communication).

It is important, however, to remember that just because you are communicating with an "internal" stakeholder, that does not mean that the information will stay "internal." Assume that all communications will become public and draft them accordingly.

Other things to consider in the response

- Photography – decide if organization videographers and photographers should take pictures of the scene for media inquiries, possible later litigation, as well as documenting events.

- Radio responses – discuss need to produce taped response for radio, or who to make available for radio sound bytes.

- Alternative communications – discuss additional means of conveying information including letters to constituencies, letters to newspaper editors, and consultation with editorial boards.

- Rumor control – consider establishing a rumor-control hotline and/or a dedicated call-in line for media use. Dedicated line also could be used for taped telephone updates.

- Scan news – television, radio, internet, print, clip and distribute, file

- Log actions and activities during crisis to be reviewed and used to improve future crisis response.

Follow Up

A communications crisis is never really complete as long as reporters and the public have memories. The press interest may have died down and the stories stopped appearing in the papers, but you are not done. Every time a similar situation occurs, the press will remember yours and may ask you about it. If prominent enough, you can expect a re-run of your story on its anniversaries and in year-end editions. Investigations can dribble out news for years. Finally, you will have to deal with the association between the organization and the image the situation and created for years to come.

As an extreme example, consider President Clinton. His "friend" is now a bonafide celebrity and every time she makes news, he makes news. For the rest of his life.

How do you know the crisis is over? The most obvious signal is that the press conference crowd dwindles to none and media calls stop coming. However, as the crisis winds down initially and the crisis team is dispersed, it is important to:

- finish out press interactions by sending promised materials, etc.;
- write thank you notes to those whose extra efforts pulled the organization through and offer leave and vacation to those affected;
- ensure that victims are counseled, cared for, and promises are kept (a terrible story if left undone); and
- follow the story to its death and beyond. News stories are like fires; you may think that they are out, but a lack of attention can burn you.

1. Before the crisis communications team breaks up, hold a post-mortem meeting to review the situation and your reactions, evaluate those actions, create a list of lessons learned, and apply them to the plan.

Rehearse, review, and revise

Finishing the plan is not the completion of the task. The plan should be tested before the first incident to analyze the effectiveness and completeness of your response.

Later, at regular intervals, retrieve the plan, assemble the principals, and walk through the scenarios looking for changes and updating as needed. Review personnel changes, alterations in procedures, corporate life changes such as public offerings, and changes in business strategy to see how they will change the planned response.

"Live" rehearsals using mock incidents will reveal weaknesses in the plan. These exercises should be scheduled at six-month intervals, if not more frequently.

Storage

Keep a paper copy of this plan and all the data therein in a sturdy, watertight notebook in a known, safe place. You might use data disks to store contact lists and such, but these should be kept with the paper copy. DO NOT commit this plan to a file server or even a laptop or PC for the simple reason that the power may be out when you need it most.

Appendices

Appendix A – key audiences

Below is a sample list of stakeholders in an organization for use in crisis communications planning. Consider these, and others, along with appropriate media when crafting the communications plan for each scenario.

Employees:
- Management
- Hourly/prospective/salaried employees
- Families
- Union members
- Retirees
- Community where employees live, neighborhood coalitions, community organizations, plant locations, Chambers of Commerce

Customer:
- Local, regional, national, and international

Functional:
- Distributors, jobbers, wholesalers, retailers, and consumers
- Industrial/Business Suppliers, teaming partners, competitors, professional societies, subcontractors, joint ventures, and trade associations

Media:
- General, local national and international; foreign trade; specialized

Investment/Financial:
- Analysts - buy and sell side
- Institutional holders, shareholders
- Bankers - commercial and investment

- Stockbrokers, portfolio managers
- Potential investors

Governmental:
- Local, state, regional, national, international
- Legislative, regulatory, executive, and judicial

Special Interests
- Environmental, safety
- Handicapped/disabled
- Minority
- Think tanks
- Consumer
- Health
- Senior citizens
- Religious.

Appendix B – sample statement

Tailor this statement to your needs and use for initial incident response

Sample News Release

A _____ at _____ involving
_____ occurred today at _____ . The incident
is under investigation and more information is forthcoming.

A (what happened) at (location) involving (who) occurred today at (time). The
incident is under investigation and more information is forthcoming.

For instance:

An explosion at 1210 Market Street, the main plant for the Acme Toy
Company occurred today at 3 p.m. The incident is under investigation and
more information is forthcoming.

- You could put down a definitive time for the next news conference or
  release of information if you know it but it is not necessary.
- You could also add information, if available, about known casualties or
  other pertinent information. This information should be definitive and not
  speculative; verify everything you say.

Appendix C – news conference checklist

Scheduling

- Check to see what else is happening in your organization or in the community before scheduling a press conference.

- Consider whether you need to let other organizations and agencies know you are having a news conference. (You may wish to invite others to attend or participate in your event.)

- Consider the news cycle, and television print deadlines, when setting a time.

- Set a time limit, but be flexible. Nothing looks worse than a spokesperson hurrying off stage under a barrage of unanswered questions.

Notification

- Notify the media by their preferred communications medium. Tell them the date, time, and exact place (add directions if necessary)

  o Give them a brief overview of what you will be announcing.

  o Notify them of any restrictions beforehand

Logistics

- Reserve a room adequate for the event. It is better to have the room too big than too small. Ensure that microphones, chairs, lighting, and water are in place at least 30 minutes prior to the event. Test all systems 15 minutes beforehand.

- Decide format in advance -- who will introduce speakers, who decides when question/answer period ends, and other details.

- Decide who will have control at the news conference, who will decide where cameras are set up, who sits where.

- Prepare handouts – proofread carefully and make sure there are more than enough. Decide whether to hand out before or after the speaker(s). If after, let the media know so that they won't take unneeded notes.

Speaker checklist

- Be at least 15 minutes early.

- Use a full script with LARGE TYPE for easy reading. You can't "wing it" or speak "off the cuff." Leave wide margin for notes to yourself. Leave pages unstapled (but numbered) for easier handling at podium. Highlight and mark your script to guide your delivery.

- Time your presentation to fit the program schedule of the group you will address.

- Practice: Read it aloud until it sounds like you are talking, not reading.

- Based on your audience and your presentation, determine what, if any, equipment you will use. If you are not familiar with the equipment, arrange a briefing on how to use slide projectors, video players, or overhead equipment.

- Check equipment (microphone, lighting, projector) and presentation in advance.

- Stand erect and direct voice toward audience, speak loudly, slowly and distinctly.

- Establish eye contact (or appear to do so) with audience from time to time.

- Stay within the allotted presentation time.

- When you are answering questions:
  - Remain friendly, cool-headed and confident.
  - Answer only the questions asked and do so as succinctly and clearly as possible.
  - Remember that you do not always have to know everything. You can say "I will have to check that out for you--please see me after the meeting.
  - Avoid allowing one person to dominate the questions by moving on: "Thank you for your interest. I'll be glad to talk to you about your concerns after the meeting. Right now let's see if anyone else has questions for the group.

- When you are finished with your presentation, remain long enough to give individuals an opportunity to talk with you and see to it that arrangements are made for distributing information materials to the group.

Appendix D – media relations guidelines

In general:

- Always return media calls and be cooperative.

- Communicate with the media -- talk to them as well as listen to them. During crisis time, you may learn a great deal from the media that can be useful to you in further dealing with the crisis.

- Avoid antagonizing the media. A short tone at a press conference, during a phone call, or elsewhere can affect your future relationship with an individual or other media who may hear the conversation.

- Consider establishing a dedicated call-in phone line that will offer information to media or others. Information on news conferences, rumour control information, newly acquired information, can be placed on a tape that can be updated. This is particularly useful when regular phone lines are tied up with calls.

- Consider how information you release to media may affect other agencies, businesses or individuals. If you say things that may result in media calling other agencies, call those agencies first to warn them of impending calls.

- When talking to the media, be sure to give credit to other agencies, groups or individuals working on the crisis, including your own staff.

- Try to be pro-active with new information. Even those things may be frantic; if you acquire new information regarding the crisis, reach out to the media.

- Be honest. Don't make false or misleading statements.

Media Interviews

General guidelines
- Do build bridges.
- Do use specifics.
- Do use analogies.
- Do use contrasts, comparisons.
- Do be enthusiastic/animated.
- Do be your casual likable self.
- Do be a listener.
- Do be cool.
- Do be correct.
- Do be anecdotal.
- If you don't have the answer or can't answer, do admit it and move on to another topic.
- Don't fall for that "A or B" dilemma.
- Don't accept "what if" questions.
- Don't accept "laundry list" questions.
- Don't go off the record.
- Don't think you have to answer every question.
- Don't speak for someone else --beware of the absent-party trap.

Broadcast:
- Prepare "talking paper" on primary points you want to make.
- Anticipate questions--prepare responses.
- Practice answering questions.
- Know who will be interviewing you, if possible.
- Determine how much time is available.
- Audiences often remember impressions, not facts. Consider the background, your dress and demeanor.

- Talk "over " lavaliere mike.
- Audio check-- use regular voice.
- If makeup is offered, use it.
- Sit far back in the chair, back erect...but lean forward to appear enthusiastic and force yourself to use hands.
- Remember... TV will frame your face--be calm, use high hand gestures, if possible.
- Keep eyes on interviewer-- not on camera.
- Smile, be friendly.
- Avoid wearing pronounced stripes, checks or small patterns.
- Grey, brown, blue or mixed colored suits/dressed are best.
- Grey, light-blue, off-white or pastel shirts or blouses are best.
- Avoid having hair cut right before interview.

Print

- Obtain advanced knowledge of interview topics.
- Make sure you are prepared in detail; print reporters are often more knowledgeable than broadcast reporters and may ask more detailed questions.
- Begin the interview by making your point in statement by making your major points in statement form.
- Try to maintain control of the interview .
- Don't let reporter wear you down.
- Set a time limit in advance.
- Don't let so relaxed that you say something you wish you hadn't.
- Avoid jargon or professional expressions.
- Reporter may repeat self in different ways to gain information you may no want to give.
- Don't answer inappropriate questions; simply say it is "not an appropriate topic for you to address at this time," or "it's proprietary" for example.
- Be prepared for interruptions with questions...it is legitimate for reporters to do that.

- Do not speak "off the record."
- Remember, the interview lasts as long as a reporter is there.

After The Interview

- You can ask to check technical points, but do not ask to see advance copy of the story.
- Never try to go over reporter's head to stop a story.
- Do not send gifts to reporters--it is considered unethical for them to accept them.

Appendix E - Web Site Crisis Communications

The Internet is now a standard corporate communications tool and a crisis communications must account for its use. The organization's stakeholders, as well as the media, will turn to the Internet for information about the situation, and will expect to see a response very quickly. To ignore this medium, to leave the home page standing as though nothing has happened, will create the impression that the organization is unresponsive and even uncaring.

A crisis can occur at any time and web site visitors will expect a quick response. However, web development takes time. Therefore, the organization should prepare "stock pages" or templates for each probable scenario and even consider keeping an entire "dark website" on reserve. These can be rapidly completed using the fact sheet and the prepared statement, reviewed and approved, and uploaded immediately to meet the need for information.

Organizations should also consider responding to external events via their websites. For instance, shortly after the terrorist attacks of September 11, 2001, many companies added memorial pages to their standard website where users could read statements of regret, be updated about the impact of the attack on the organization and its communities of stakeholders, offer condolences, and make contributions. For example:

- UPS provided status updates about package deliveries.

- Yahoo supplied information about how to help out by donating blood and assisting victims families.

- Microsoft and other corporate web sites added a message of condolence.

- EBay announced a special "Auction For America."

Stock pages or templates

- Templates used during a communications crisis should have simple navigation and small file sizes (few and simple graphics) to speed download and reduce server loads.

- Content should be coded with simple html for easy additions and edits to speed development.

- Headlines should be html, not graphical, for speed, to reduce server loads, and to ease updating.
- The crisis pages may be placed outside of the main content area and provide links to the regular web site, especially if the normal site is complex.
- Don't use server side code and avoid the use of Flash or other plug-ins that may slow downloads or require the user to download and install software to see the content.
- Show the date and time of the last update to let users see how current is the information.
- Don't use pop-ups; they are often ignored and may even be blocked by the browser.
- Have back-up servers available to ensure continuity.
- Allow users to sign up for e-mail updates and post telephone numbers and e-mail addresses they can use to get more information.
- Stress test your server and increase its capacity by adding RAM to your server, reducing the number of hops across the Internet, using a separate server for emergency content only, using caching technology to only serve up content elements the user hasn't seen, and shortening the distance between your users and Internet connection (i.e. global firms may wish to locate a server overseas).

Crisis Communications Workbook

General guidelines

1. Describe your organization's general policy for crisis communications.

Planning

1. List your organization's set of scenarios; a series of probable situations that would require a public response (to reduce this number, group situations by type and use a generic scenario).

2. For each scenario above, create a list of stakeholders and their respective communications channels for each scenario. You will need to aggregate these lists, ensure that contact information is up-to-date, and store them (paper copies) with the crisis communications plan.

3. Walk through each scenario described above and determine probable and possible ramifications of the situation. Use these lists to define "packages" of materials needed to respond to the incident (keep paper copies of these packages in with the crisis communications plan).

These packages might include:

- a draft position and key messages;

- a draft statement (see appendix X for a sample);

- lists of key stakeholders for the scenario and their contact information;

- anticipated questions and answers;

- third-party experts (and contact information); and

- a fact sheet on the operation or process involved, including schematics and photos if possible.

4. Use the criteria in the handbook to identify the Crisis Communications team.

5. Create a recall roster for every member of the team and their alternates. List their:

- Name,
- Title,
- Role and responsibility on the team,
- Department or division,
- Telephone numbers for work, home, and cell,
- Fax numbers,
- IM address, and e-mail address.

Keep this roster up-to-date and keep a paper copy of this list with the crisis communications plan.

6. List the specific crisis communications tasks of the public affairs staff and the responsible person.

7. Use the criteria in the handbook to designate a spokesperson and a back-up and train them in media relations.

8. Identify a command center, a press center, and a family center, as well as alternates, and the person responsible for (has the key to) each room. List each room's capacity, physical layout, and location. List the equipment needed in each facility for the crisis. If the equipment would need to be obtained, list the person responsible for the equipment and their work, home, and cell telephone numbers.

Response

Create a step-by-step process to guide the initial response to the situation.

Sample response steps

1. Activate the plan, recall and assemble the team, create a fact sheet, and develop a position on the situation.

2. Use the fact sheet and the positioning to write, clear, and release a brief, factual statement about the situation.

3. Determine media interest and the appropriate responses.

4. Use the press conference checklist to prepare; ensure you rehearse expected questions and answers, review guidelines, and coordinate the release of information among the parties involved.

5, Use the most applicable scenario package to develop collateral press materials to give to the press, to develop communications internally and with stakeholders.

6. Create and maintain a media and a public contact log, noting for each interaction, the:

- Date;
- Name;
- Title;
- Company;
- Telephone number of caller;
- Questions(s) asked;
- Person responsible for response;
- Additional follow-up needs.

Follow-up

Note the following in the plan:

- Exercise log – when, who, what, summary of results.
- Document revision history to log the date, place, and type of revision.

About the author

Matthew Montague is the Director of Public Relations for Smith Marketing Services of Ithaca, NY. He has more than 15 years of experience in marketing and media relations. Specific to crisis communications, he has written plans for and executed high-profile media events for the US Navy (aircraft crashes, training accidents, and wartime deployments and operations), managed media for political campaigns and very large conference events, handled press for a corporate merger, overseen investor communications, and driven media relations for a dot com start-up. He has international experience in England, France, Italy, Turkey, Iraq, Israel, Switzerland, Germany, Finland, and Norway. For more information, please see www.onlinesms.com.

Notes

Notes

<u>Notes</u>

Made in the USA
Lexington, KY
16 January 2013